LONCROSS PRESS

The von Blumenthals at Gravelotte

Henry von Blumenthal was born in 1961. He was educated at Westminster School and Christ Church, Oxford, where he read Theology. For ten years he worked in the City for oriental stockbrokers. From 1996-2000 he lived in Moscow as an advisor to the City of Moscow on its debt; for a year after that he worked in Bulgaria for the government of the ex-King Simeon II as an advisor on Capital Markets. Since 2001 he has lived with his wife and two children in Luxembourg, where he is Deputy Dean of the EIB Institute.

Also published by Longcross Press are his *Prussia, the Junker Point of View* and *Seven Stories for Christmas,* as well as *The Companion to British History* by his late father Charles Arnold-Baker, of which he is the editor.

The von Blumenthals

at

Gravelotte

August 1870

by

Henry von Blumenthal

LONGCROSS PRESS

Published by Longcross Press

Lameschmillen, L 3316, Luxembourg

Copyright © Henry von Blumenthal, 2016
The moral right of the author has been asserted.

ISBN 978-9995954000

**For Alexis,
with love**

Only when one is a father oneself is it possible to understand the feelings of those fathers who lost a son in battle.

CONTENTS

			Page
Introduction			
I.		Preliminaries: Vionville – Mars-la-Tour	13
	a.	Oskar 1st. Hanoverian Dragoons, No. 9	13
	b.	Georg	17
	c.	Werner, 1st Dragoon Guards	23
II.		Gravelotte – St. Privat	33
	d.	Vally, Ordnanzoffizier with Gen. von Steinmetz	33
	e.	Maximilian, Colonel, and Erich, 73rd Fusiliers	36
	f.	Gustav	38
	g.	Maximilian, 2nd Dragoon Guards	43
	h.	Arthur	44
	i.	Werner, the Hussar	44

Tables, Maps and Illustrations:

Oskar, Rittmeister, 1st. Hanoverian Dragoons No. 9	13
A dragoon of the 1st. Hanoverian Dragoons No. 9	15
Georg	17
General von Doering	21
General von Bredow receives the order to charge	22
Colonel von Auerswald	24
The Charge of the 1st Dragoon Guards	26
Col. von Auerswald raises a cheer for the King	27
Prince Friedrich von Hohenzollern-Sigmaringen	28
Map: the von Blumenthals at Gravelotte	30
Family tree: the von Blumenthals at Gravelotte	21
Vally, Blücher Hussars, and Cornelia	35
Maximilian, Lt. Colonel of the 73rd Fusiliers	37
Maximilian, 2nd Dragoon Guards	43

Bibliography   48

Introduction

In the 1950s a group of elderly gentlemen was overheard in the Oxford and Cambridge Club deploring the shortness of public memory. One of them said indignantly in a high falsetto "Nowadays, hardly anyone remembers the Franco-Prussian War!"

So it was then, so it is today. Since the fall of the Soviet Empire, the public has grudgingly accepted that history did not begin in October 1917 but in fact three years earlier, at the start of the First World War rather than at its end.

This modest concession does not alter the fact that anyone determined to fix a date for the beginning of the modern era must at least "remember the Franco-Prussian War," for both its military and its political developments.

Here we find the first railway mobilisation, the first use in Europe of the machine gun, the first military use of aerial flight (balloons). But the political developments are what really catch the attention. The results of the war were the death of the monarchical ideal, in Germany no less than in France. On the German side, the new Kaiser wept as he signed the proclamation which he knew spelled the end of his own kingdom. On the French side, republican ideologues were able to override the democratically expressed demand for a return of the Bourbons, and put an end to the dreams of French monarchists forever. Meanwhile, the experiment of the Paris Commune became a prototype for future soviets.

Gravelotte was the pivotal battle of the war. France had already lost several battles and would lose more, but her last chance depended on the possibility of uniting the two big armies at Metz and Châlons. In a nutshell, what happened was this: Bazaine led his army out from Metz towards Châlons. As they marched down the Route Imperiale they were attacked from the left between Vionville and Mars-la-Tour. The road thus changed from being the French line of march to the French line of disposition.

While this was happening, the columns who had left Metz last were unable to move on and so took a rightwards, more northerly route behind their comrades as the latter were still fighting. When they reached a part of the road between Gravelotte and St. Private they also faced left, and started preparing what would become the fallback position of those already fighting the Germans.

This prepared position was not without merit and it was by no means certain that the Germans could win an outright assault on the whole French army now entrenched here. Of course, with hindsight, they should have just marched on to Châlons.

This is not, however, a straightforward description of the battle, but an account of how it looked from the perspective of ten members of my tiny family who took part. That so many close relatives should fight on the same field is a comment on the interesting way the old Prussian Junker system worked. Every Prussian nobleman was expected to fight and possibly die in battle. Those who went into the civil service or looked after their estates never really felt they were performing their role properly. They were the poorest aristocracy in Europe and the most selfless, and in a state in which all the decision makers were soldiers, it followed that the officers had to have other talents besides. Often they were poets, artists, farmers or politicians. It is fun to laugh at Prussian militarism with its spiked hats and jackboots, but this militarism brought universal free education and state health to Germany a century before democracy brought it to Britain.

The format of this book is thus conceived as a survey of the roles of my ten relatives in the two battles. As they were in all the key actions of both, this makes a coherent narrative of the battles themselves. I also say something in each case about their background and how they were related to each other. There is a map and family tree linked by numerical references to help with this.

I hope therefore that this booklet can be of both military and social interest, not least to my own posterity.

I. Preliminaries; Vionville-Mars la Tour

a. Oskar

Rittmeister Count Oskar von Blumenthal of the 1st Hanoverian Dragoon Regiment No. 9. He commanded the patrol which discovered the exit of Bazaine from Metz. He fought at both Vionville and Gravelotte.

In a sense it was a von Blumenthal who precipitated the successive battles of Vionville-Mars la Tour and Gravelotte-St. Privat. The Emperor Napoleon III's army had been driven back from the German frontier into Metz, pursued by the German Second Army. The Emperor handed over command to Marshal Bazaine with orders to join the French army at Châlons, and departed. It was 15th. August, the Feast of the Assumption, and the Emperor's birthday, which the French had optimistically scheduled for a victory parade in Berlin.

It was not obvious to the Germans what Bazaine was going to do; at first it looked as if he planned to make a stand before Metz, but the Germans were methodical in their scouting methods and sent out cavalry patrols to investigate. One of these, commanded by Rittmeister Count Oskar von Blumenthal, made its way in an anti-clockwise arc around Metz to the north, systematically entering villages and questioning the inhabitants. Eventually at Ars he found a frightened schoolmaster who had just come out of Metz, who said that "fifty thousand French troops had left Metz the previous evening taking the route Langeville, Moulins, Ste Ruffine, and the Route Imperiale through Gravelotte, Vionville and Mars la Tour."

Oskar was 36, the second of four surviving children. When he was 17 he had cut short his schooling to join the Prussian Dragoon Guards, where his father, Count Bernhard commanded a squadron. The 1850s were peaceable times and his elder sister Asta von Pachelbl had married her first husband the same year. She widowed young and by now had just remarried to another cavalry officer in very different times; her new husband Friedrich von

Pachelbl was also on campaign. There was another sister, Olga, still only 19; and his brother Count Alfons had only just returned to his regiment, the 7th King's Grenadiers, after having been badly wounded in the Austro-Prussian War. He was somewhere to the south, in the 3rd. Army which his cousin Leonhardt, General, later Field Marshal and currently Chief of Staff of the Crown Prince.

A dragoon of the 1st Hanoverian Dragoon Regiment No. 9 from Richard Knötel's famous series of illustrations of uniforms.

Oskar was by now a seasoned fighter. After receiving his full commission he had been transferred to the 1st Silesian Dragoons and was on the staff of the German high command during the first of Bismarck's wars, against Denmark in 1863-4. The Prussians had been the first to develop methodical staffwork and to treat war as a much more intellectual process than hitherto. After the Danish war he was adjutant of a cavalry brigade but when the Austro-Prussian War broke out in 1866 out he was on the Staff of the 2nd. Army under Leonhardt, who had been Chief of Staff also in that war. Oskar had seen plenty of action against the Austrians; he fought at the battles of Trautenau, Skalitz, Königinhof, Schweinschädel and the decisive victory at Königgrätz, where his brother was so badly wounded.

The following year he had married Wanda von Knobelsdorff, a colonel's daughter, though the marriage was childless and would end in divorce a decade later.

Oskar had been decorated with the Order of the Red Eagle and given command of the 1st Squadron of the 9th Dragoons, as a reward for his conduct in the war against Austria. It was this squadron which now had in its hands the frightened schoolmaster of Ars, and it was Oskar who questioned him. It looked as if the French had escaped. Oskar's report, which earned him the Iron Cross (IInd. Class), reached Prince Frederick Charles of Prussia, the "Red Prince," commanding the Prussian Second Army, that same night.

b. Georg

Lt. Georg von Blumenthal of the 8th Grenadiers, Deputy Adjutant of the Prussian 9th Brigade. He survived the battles of Vionville and Gravelotte but was mortally wounded in the 3-day Battle of Orleans in December 1870. His was the last face his dying commander saw.

To catch at least the tail-end of the retreating French, the Red Prince despatched General von Alvensleben's IIIrd Corps, 30,000 men from Brandenburg, among them the young Lt. Georg von

Blumenthal of the 8th Grenadiers, who was barely 20.

Georg and his brother Curt were Leonhardt's nephews, sons of his brother Louis, who was also a general. He was now retired but had seen action in all the Prussian army's wars up to that point since the Berlin insurrection in 1848, but was now retired, living mostly with the family of his wife, Louisa von Burgsdorff at their estate at Hohenjesar, together with their young son Hans. Louis' grandfather - Louisa's great-grandfather - Werner von Blumenthal had been a colonel in Frederick the Great's time, and his father had been killed in a squadron charge in the Napoleonic Wars at Dennewitz.

The two brothers were separated in different armies, Georg in the Third, Curt in the Second, but had seen their first action on the same day in different battles less than 10 days before, on 6th August, at Spicheren and Wörth respectively. At Wörth, a victory which Leonhardt had masterminded, Curt had been badly wounded and had spent the whole night on the bare earth shivering under a French horse-blanket, having directed the stretcher party to attend to one of his men first. The Crown Prince noted in his diary that, riding over the field of victory next day he had seen him there. He was now on the mend at home and hoping to rejoin the fighting.

Georg, Curt and their cousin Friedrich had all been at the cadet school in Berlin together. Georg's regiment was brigaded with the 48th Foot to form the 9th Infantry Brigade under Major General von Döring, and Georg was the deputy adjutant of the brigade, itself part of General von Stülpnagel's 5th Infantry Division.

The 3rd. Corps got close to the *Route Imperiale* and bivouacked for what was left of the night, sending out patrols to watch for the French. There were indeed troops still coming out of Metz, but it was impossible to tell if these were the rearguard or the van.

In the small hours General von Alvensleben headed towards the route to Châlons near Vionville. Standing on the plateau, he realised that the 50,000 troops which Oskar had reported were in fact the vanguard, with behind them the whole of the French Army whose departure from Metz had been delayed by inward-bound heavy baggage.

Notwithstanding the odds, the gallant von Alvensleben attacked. The battle developed along the road between Vionville and Mars-la-Tour, as more and more troops on both sides got sucked into the action.

The English *Daily News* reported: "*The plain on which the battle was fought extends from the woods to the Verdun road, about one mile and a half, and is about three miles in length. On the French right the ground rises gently, and this was the key of the position, as the artillery, which would maintain itself there, swept the whole field. . . . From the woods to Rezonville, on the Verdun road, there is no cover, except one cottage midway on the Gorze road. This cottage was held by a half battery of French mitrailleuses, which did frightful execution in the Prussian ranks as they advanced from the wood.*"

This battle was marked by two Prussian cavalry charges, von Bredow's memorable Death Ride, and the less well-remembered but no less glorious charge of the Prussian Dragoon Guards, though the Infantry and Artillery can hardly be said to have made less effort than the cavalry.

Georg was one of the 15,000 Prussians who now struggled across this plain against the heights on the French right, which had been hastily strengthened by an earthwork. They were raked by the French mitrailleuse battery as they repeatedly attempted to take the key position. Baffled and repulsed, the Prussians still persisted, until after three hours they drove the French off. Up the hill the Prussian horse artillery raced as the French artillery were galloping away to a hill on the right. They were only 500 yards apart, and for a long time a duel ensued between the two artilleries in their new positions. The carnage was dreadful. At last the French guns moved off once more, to another hill farther off, so the Prussians immediately took up their vacant position.

General von Buddenbrock's 6th. Division, made up of Brandenburgers, advanced toward Mars-la-Tour, wheeled to the right, and, in the face of a rain of shot and shell, carried Flavigny and pushed on toward Vionville.

Major-General von Döring, commander of the 9th Infantry Brigade, who died in Georg's arms at the Battle of Vionville.

The 9th and 10th brigades in von Stülpnagel's 5th Infantry division had been amalgamated in the struggle. It *"fought its way to the front with desperate courage, but with varying fortune. One regiment in particular—the 52nd (formerly commanded by*

Georg's father) —*lost heavily in recovering some ground which had been wrested from it by the French. Its first battalion lost every one of its officers; the colours were passed from hand to hand as the bearers were successively shot down by the bullets of the chassepots, and the commander of the brigade, General von Döring fell mortally wounded."* As von Döring's Deputy Adjutant, Georg was walking just behind the general. Cradling his commander in his arms, he watched him die, and then, after ordering the body to be carried to the rear, resumed the advance with the brigade. For this coolness under fire he won the Iron Cross (IInd. Class).

General von Bredow receives the order to charge from the personal hand of Colonel Voigts-Rhetz

As the fighting wore on, General von Alvensleben realised that a determined French attack would result in defeat. He ordered Gen. von Bredow's 12th Cavalry Brigade to forestall the French attack and silence the guns. Placing himself at the head of six squadrons of Uhlans and Cuirassiers, von Bredow cried *"Koste es, was es wolle!"* – "Cost what it may!"

and launched his famous Death Ride, which swept the French artillery away, drove off their cavalry, and returned, having lost half its numbers. The success of this charge ensured the place of cavalry as an executive arm in modern armies for another half century.

c. Werner of the 1ˢᵗ Dragoon Guards

The French fell back, or rather, fell forward towards Châlons, on Mars-la-Tour. At about 1 p.m. General von Voigts-Rhetz's 10ᵗʰ Corps at last started to arrive to take up position in defence of the ground before Mars-la-Tour. First in line were the light infantry (Jägers), who started peppering Le Boeuf's advancing French at Tronville. But the exhausted men of the 6ᵗʰ Division wavered. Seeing them fall back, General von Voigts-Rhetz decided to commit his remaining cavalry to a charge, and gave the order to General von Brandenburg. All he had were the 1ˢᵗ. Dragoon Guards and two squadrons of the 4ᵗʰ. Cuirassiers. These had been hovering between the village of Ville-sur-Yron and the extreme right of the French position, in order to block a flanking charge from some French cavalry which were seen somewhat back and to the right of the French right flank proper.

Colonel von Auerswald of the 1st Dragoon Guards, Werner von Blumenthal's commander, mortally wounded at Mars-la-Tour

The Dragoons' Colonel von Auerswald led them back to behind the village of Mars-la-Tour and formed them up. The 4th. Squadron was placed in reserve, behind the village. It was commanded by Rittmeister Prince Friedrich von Hohenzollern-Sigmaringen - brother of King Carol I of Roumania. He was a close friend in the regiment of Werner.

This Werner was the son of Count Werner von Blumenthal; his mother had died after giving birth to him in 1848. Unlike Oskar and Alfons, whose title of Count could be inherited by all their sons in their lifetime, this branch of the family held the title on condition that it could only be inherited by the eldest son on the death of his father, and only so long as they continued to own the beautiful estate of Suckow. Unfortunately the King compulsorily purchased Suckow, so that young Werner inherited neither the title nor the estate. But these troubles were in the future.

In the excitement of war with Austria, he had broken off his school education, taken the ensign's exam and rushed to the front as a volunteer in the First Dragoon Guards, much like his distant cousin Oskar some years before. The very day he joined up he was off to the front. At Königgrätz he was in the charge against the Austrian 11th Uhlans which resulted in a famous cavalry mêlée. He was commissioned in the field and was now a 2nd lieutenant.

Now it was time for another charge. It was clear that few would return, and General von Brandenburg called out to Colonel von Auerswald "I'm coming too!" As they rode out from behind Mars-la-Tour and lined up for the charge with the village on their left, it burst into flames sparked by French shelling. They formed up due north of the burning Mars-la-Tour, facing Le Boeuf's infantry. Then they set off at a walk down either side of the road to Bruville. Passing through the Prussian 5th Jägers, they began to be shot at by the French 57th Regiment ahead and the 13th and 43rd Regiments to their right, as well as shelled by the artillery.

They wheeled right and charged the 13th. After that they regrouped and, heading leftwards, they overran the 57th. This halted the French advance on the still half-assembled Prussian left flank, but the suicidal attack cost the regiment nine officers killed, four wounded and one captured. Two of Bismarck's sons, both troopers, were in the charge. Herbert, the elder, was wounded; his brother saved a comrade's life.

The charge of the 1st Dragoon Guards at Mars-la-Tour. The central figure is Heinrich, Prince Reuss, of the 5th Squadron, who commissioned the painting by Emil Hünten

Covered in blood, Colonel von Auerswald led the survivors back from the charge round the other side of Mars-la-Tour to where the reserve 4th. Squadron was waiting and then, assembling them around him, addressed them: "Dragoons, you rode in well and bravely, I am delighted with you all; I am mortally wounded. God save his Majesty the King!" He died five days later.

Colonel von Auerswald, mortally wounded, thanks the men of the 1st Dragoon Guards and raises a cheer for the King.

As the senior surviving officer, Rittmeister von Hohenzollern now took command of the regiment; he led the 4th. Squadron and the remnants of the other squadrons back into action for a final charge.

General von Rheinbaben now arrived with the 5th Cavalry Division, which he launched on the French flank in the grassy fields between the village and a stream called the Yron. The ensuing massed cavalry mêlée lasted to nightfall. It would still have been possible for the French to escape to Châlons, but

Rittmeister Prince Friedrich von Hohenzollern-Sigmaringen - brother of King Carol I of Roumania. He and Werner were close friends in the 1st. Dragoon Guards and took part in the famous dragoon charge at Mars-la-Tour. After the war they travelled together to Egypt, Greece and Turkey.

Bazaine ordered the troops who had been engaged at Mars-la-Tour to fall back on his main army at Gravelotte. For this order, French conspiracy theorists would soon accuse him of treason, not only to his Emperor, whose fate could already be guessed, but to France herself. It is more probable that he was gripped by the same mental paralysis which had afflicted the entire French high command from the beginning. He was also fat and sluggish; but it had nothing to do with cowardice for he did not shrink from the next, much greater, battle.

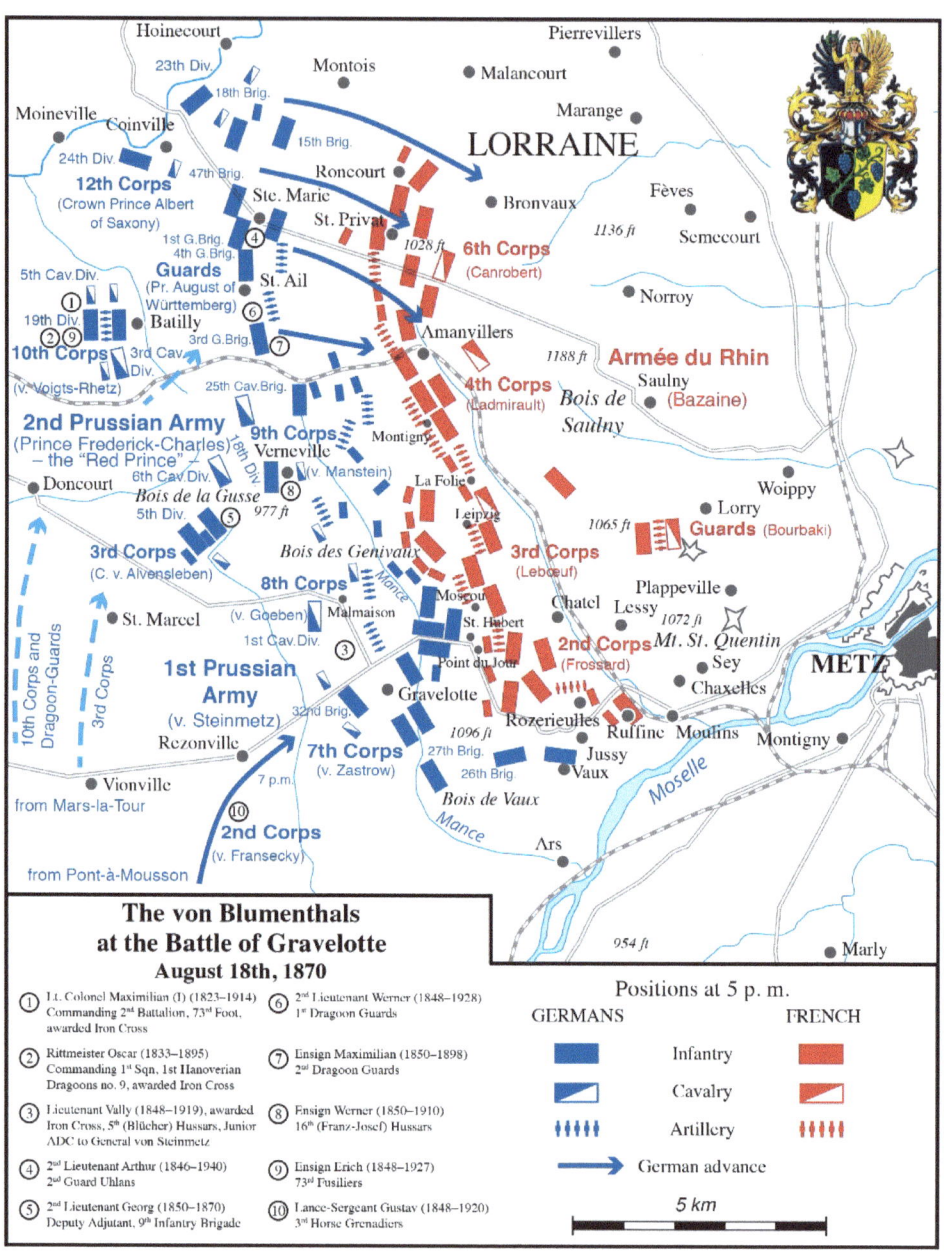

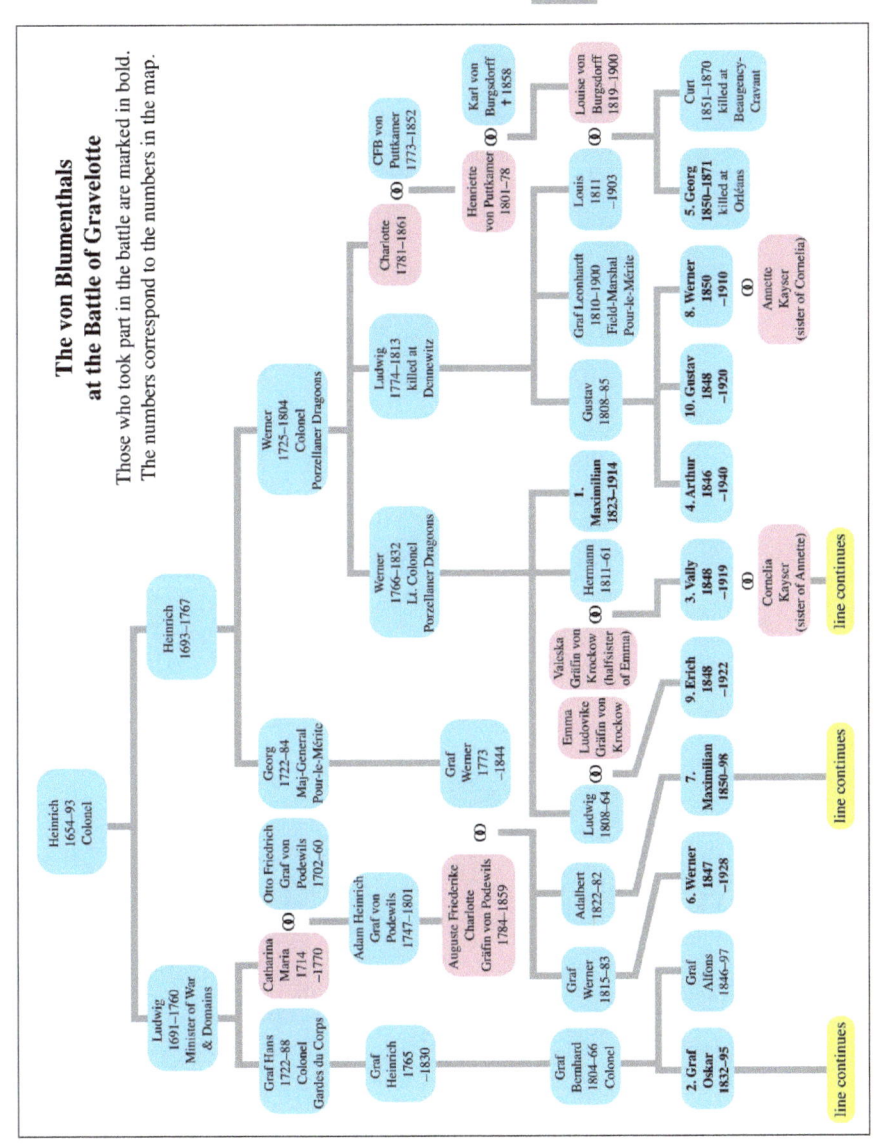

II. Gravelotte – St. Privat

The battle of Gravelotte came about on 18th August 1870 when the commander of the German 2nd. Army, Prince Frederick Charles, known as the Red Prince due his fondness for a red uniform, not his political ideas, ordered an advance on the French position. This meant that the men had to step over dead bodies in the ploughed fields before Mars-la-Tour where they had just fought. Artillery drivers could hear skulls cracking under the wheels. This time each side knew roughly where the other was, though the Red Prince at first thought he was chasing the rearguard of the French, whom he assumed to be falling back on Metz. It was only when General von Moltke came onto the scene and the various Prussian forces (apart from the Crown Prince's 3rd. Army) concentrated, that the fact the French had a prepared position became evident. The ten Blumenthals who would fight at the great struggle of Gravelotte-St. Privat would be present on almost every part of it.

d. <u>Vally</u>

General von Steinmetz was in command of the First Army, and now for the first time was with it at the front. Vally was transferred to his staff a few days before the battle as *Ordnanzoffizier*, a Junior ADC. Vally's unusual Christian name was chosen by his heartbroken father Herrmann after his beloved wife Valeska von Krockow died giving birth to their only child. Herrmann had been one of five brothers and four sisters. Of the brothers Robert, Maximilian, Ludwig and Hermann, the latter two were distinguished. The fifth, Wilhelm, died as a cadet aged 17. Of the sisters, only one married, to an infantry captain. The eldest brother, Robert, became the longest-serving governor of Danzig in history, during a turbulent period. The youngest, Maximilian, became a Major-General and took part in this battle as a battalion commander. Hermann himself, after twenty years' peacetime service in a run-of-the-mill infantry regiment, never made it to captain. He left the army after his wife's death and became reclusive, living in Pomerania, mostly in Stolp either at his mother Louise (née von Hartmann)'s house, or sometimes at the nearby estate of Schlönwitz which he acquired through his wife's inheritance, until he died when Vally was 17. Left in the hands of his maiden aunts Vally lacked male company and was left to fend largely for himself. Bismarck, whose wife was a friend of the von Blumenthal family, was sorry for the lad and used to have him over on Sundays, and thus called him "My 'Sunday's Child'" (*Mein Sonntagskind*).

Lt. Vally von Blumenthal, of the Blücher Hussars, wearing the Iron Cross he won at Gravelotte, with his wife Cornelia (née Kayser) whom he married two years after the war.

He joined the Lichtenfeld Corps of Cadets in Berlin and went into the Blücher Hussars in 1866 just in time to go to war against Austria. He fought at Münchengrätz, at the furious engagement at Gitschin and at Königgrätz where he was commissioned in the field. He remembered that six-week war as a "picnic": "We all got hatfuls of medals and no-one was killed." Gravelotte was to be his first action in this war.

Vally's task during the battle was to bear the momentous orders of General von Steinmetz to those who had to carry them out. In between, he was able to observe the development of the battle from the point by the village of Gravelotte where von Steinmetz and his staff established themselves.

e. Maximilian, the Fusilier Colonel, and Erich

On the right wing, in the woods to the right of Gravelotte, which lay on part of the previous day's battlefield, in front of Ars, were the 73rd Fusiliers, where Vally's uncle Maximilian and cousin Erich were serving. As a Lt. Colonel, Maximilian commanded his battalion while his late brother Ludwig's polite and delicate 22-year-old son Erich carried the colour as ensign.

Maximilian's father had been a colonel of dragoons during the Napoleonic Wars. He himself had been a major commanding a company of the 1st Grenadiers during the Austro-Prussian War where he had fought at Trautenau and Königgrätz and been rewarded with the Order of the Red Eagle and command of a battalion of the 73rd Fusiliers. By now he was 47 and had only two years before married Thekla von Puttkamer; they lived on her estate at Grünwalde but so far had no children. For his nephew Erich, Gravelotte would be his first and last action, for though he lived into the late 1920s, he fell ill after the battle and retired from the army.

The regiment was connected via the Mance Valley with 8th. Corps, which Moltke had transferred from the First to the Second Army, and occupied Gravelotte itself. Behind, 2nd. Corps occupied the village of Rezonville.

Lt. Colonel Maximilian von Blumenthal, commander of the 2nd Battalion, 73rd Fusiliers. At Gravelotte he led his battalion up the Mance Ravine through a murderous cross-fire only to be bombarded by mistake by Prussian artillery.

f. Gustav

Slightly behind Rezonville were the 3rd Dragoons, where the most junior member of the family, Gustav was a lance-serjeant, shortly to be commissioned for bravery in the face of the enemy.

Gustav was another nephew of Leonhardt's and thus the first cousin of Georg and Curt. His father Gustav had been medically disqualified from the army despite having scored the top marks at the Cadet School in Berlin; and had then had to watch his brothers Ludwig and Leonhardt follow glittering military careers. To some extent he made up by being equally brilliant at managing his family properties, to which he added enormously, so that by the end of the 1870s he owned the estates of Segenthin (where the younger Gustav was born), Deutsch-Puddiger, Vehlow and Tonowo. Now three of the elder Gustav's four sons were about to see action, the fourth being too young.

Young Gustav had not entirely intended to pursue a military career. Although he went to Cadet School and served in the army as a part-time volunteer, encouraged by his uncle Leonhardt, he was really being groomed to manage his father's estates. However, when war loomed in 1870 he signed up and went to the front, as did his brothers Arthur and Werner, who were in this battle.

In this part of the line, the stench of rotting corpses from the previous day was nauseating.

Further over to the left, at a distance of about four miles, 3rd. Corps occupied the Prussian centre, nestling among the woods, resting their left flank on the village of Verneville. Here stood the 9th Brigade, where Georg was now adjutant to a new commander.

On the left wing, at first facing the forward French position at St Marie, in front of St Privat, was the Corps of Guards, which was taking the ground in the approach to the nearer village of St. Ail. Out of sight to the left was the Saxon Corps, whose objective was to outflank the French right. The original intention was simply to encircle them and contain them. However, it did not become apparent, until after the attack on the French left had started, how very far the French right extended, and this forced the Saxons into a longer and more tiring march than expected, also causing delays in the development of the Guards' attack on Ste. Marie.

The French faced the Prussians from higher ground sloping up from a rivulet called the Mance. To their left, this flowed through a steep dip known as the Mance Ravine; to their right the slope was more and more gentle, though still enough to make walking up it tiring. The French rear was up against a convenient road and railways, making communications easy, but retreat was difficult because it was blocked by the Moselle. They had set up field fortifications and entrenchments which incorporated a string of farm buildings, at Jussy, Point du Jour, St. Hubert, Moscou (named after the events of 1812), Leipzig (after 1806), La Follie, Montigny la Grange and the villages of Amanvillers and St. Privat.

At the last minute, on the other side of the Mance, they had occupied Ste. Marie, a solidly built place with excellent walls, but which they failed to make properly defensible with barricades. Before most of the French lines lay open ground, the gentle slope up from the Mance acting like "a natural open glacis" as the American General Sheridan, who was there, observed.

The Prussian high command was unsure what to do next. General von Roon argued that attacking here would achieve nothing; the French were already cut off from their supplies and, once the Saxons had gone round, would soon be surrounded. As before, events were decided lower down the hierarchy. General von Manstein started an artillery duel in the centre and directed his 18th division to get ready for an advance. His guns worked forward with the infantry towards Moscou, but the return fire was deadly.

Old General von Steinmetz heard the cannonade and now committed an unforgivable act of insubordination. Setting up his headquarters at Gravelotte, a village across the Mance from the farm of Moscou, he not only recklessly sent VII Corps to support von Manstein's assault, he also sent in von Gröben's VIII Corps, which he no longer commanded. They brought their artillery to bear, enfilading the French lines and taking the pressure off von Manstein's guns. So far so good. But now von Gröben's two principal divisons, the 15th and 16th, were brought up. The 15th. started forward, and before long was taking terrible casualties.

Then VII Corps came up. It was Vally's task to carry von Steinmetz' orders to the units and send them on their way. He was able to watch his cousins Maximilian and Erich's regiment, the 73rd Fusiliers, as it toiled up the cobbled path from Gravelotte before descending into the Mance Ravine. From here, it was an uphill march into the thick of the French defences between Moscou and Point du Jour. It was a cross-fire of Mitrailleuses, Chassepot and canister. The Corps wavered and fled. Seeing this, the King himself rode down with General Sheridan and Moltke. Passing through Gravelotte, they ran into General von Steinmetz, roughly where the

Gravelotte Museum now stands, opposite the German war memorial. "Why are the men retreating?" demanded the King, who had been swearing at the fugitives as he passed them. "Their officers are all dead, Your Majesty." Tempers were flaring, and the King said the fleeing men were all cowards. Moltke would not have this. "But Your Majesty, "he exclaimed, "they are dying for you like heroes." "I'll be the judge of that," said the King, who was certainly no coward himself. Moltke angrily turned his horse round and left the King, practically alone in the foremost part of the front. Perhaps the King saw that von Steinmetz was exaggerating, for there were still plenty of officers fit for duty – neither Maximilian nor his nephew Erich had been hurt, for example.

At the other end of the line, the Prussians were still forming up. The Guards were ready around Amanvillers, waiting for the Saxons. At about the time von Steinmetz's Corps was in mid-flight, the Guards and Saxons began a tremendous bombardment on the French right at St. Privat. The Guards were preparing to take Ste Marie, so as to create a link with the Saxons, and seeing this the French sallied out to take the unoccupied village of St. Ail. There was a race for it, which the Guard Light Infantry won; then they took Ste Marie.

g. Maximilian of the Dragoon Guards

From here the Guards formed up to face the French around St. Privat squarely. Behind the village were the 3rd Guards Cavalry Brigade, consisting of the 1st and 2nd Dragoon Guards, where Werner, who had already fought at Vionville the day before, and his cousin Maximilian were respectively serving.

Ensign Maximilian von Blumenthal of the 2nd Hanoverian Dragoon Guards

Maximilian's father Adalbert was the younger brother of Werner's father, Count Werner. He was born at the charming estate of Varzin, which the von Blumenthals later sold to Bismarck, had been mostly educated at home and had only joined the army the year before aged 19.

h. Arthur

Just behind Werner and Maximilian in the Dragoons were the 2nd Guard Uhlans, where Arthur was a 2nd lieutenant, in a hollow by St. Ail, occupying the ground between the Guards and 10th Corps.

Arthur was Gustav's brother and was born in Berlin in the family home of his mother, Anna von Arnim in 1846. He went into the 1st. Foot Guards aged 20 and took part in the war against Austria. He fought at Soor and Königinhof. Then at Königrätz he was wounded in the head by a grenade splinter during the celebrated storming of the heights of Chlum, and was decorated. After the Austrian War he transferred to the cavalry and was now in a squadron of the Uhlans, stationed only slightly in front of Oskar's regiment, the 9th Dragoon Guards, formed up beside the village of Batilly.

i. Werner, the Hussar

The Saxon 12th. Corps began to appear on the extreme left, enfilading the French around Roncourt.

Here Gustav and Arthur's brother, Werner (not to be confused with his cousin Werner in the Dragoon Guards) carried the colour of the 16th Hussars. Too young to have fought in the Austro-Prussian War, this was his first action.

This was the moment when the outcome of the battle hung in the balance. If the French followed up their success at Gravelotte, they would win; if not, they would lose at St. Privat. The Guards' artillery now came to bear on the French positions, and the combined effect of the bombardment from both Prussian armies was terrible, a foretaste of the Trenches of WWI and the Blitz of WWII. Even today, the local expression for heavy rain is "raining like Gravelotte."

The French artillery did not make it easy for the Prussian gunners, who had to work forward, limbering up and unlimbering again. Anyone who has seen the Royal Horse Artillery firing the Queen's Salute at Hyde Park can imagine how exhausting this was. The ammunition wagons had also to be brought up and the supply of shells synchronised. On the right wing, it was Vally's task as junior ADC to ensure the details, riding back and forth under fire to see that the roads were kept clear by other units, who were themselves eager to press along. For this work he earned the Iron Cross.

Marshal Canrobert, commanding the St. Privat position, was alarmed to see the Saxons arriving on his right, but Bazaine ignored his pleas for supplies and reinforcements. Many of his guns were now out of action, but this proved a godsend to the French, for the silence of his artillery tempted General von Württemberg to launch the Guards into a premature attack. The defenders concentrated on them until they began to reel; officers had to drive their men back into the fight at sword point. But then at last the Saxons engaged, and the French right wing collapsed, unbelievably, because twenty men per company were detached to cook dinner!

As the French right cracked, so did the centre; but even now victory was not assured. The 7th. and 8th. Corps were exhausted and suffering heavily from the struggle up the Mance Ravine. Maximilian and Erich's unit, the 73rd Fusiliers, was caught in a cross-fire which was now made worse by Prussian guns arriving at Gravelotte who bombarded the whole area, unaware that their own men were mixed into the French position. Panic started to set in, and for the second time knots of Prussian soldiers ran back past their own king shouting "All is lost!" This did not, however, go for Maximilian's battalion, which stood firm and earned him the Iron Cross (II Class). The king believed them, unaware that though this part of the Prussian line was falling back, the entire French army was on the run. The only French who stayed put did so out of fear of leaving their shelters. Once again in Prussian military history, the Leuthen Chorale, whose melody had been composed two centuries before by Johannes Crüger, the house-tutor of the von Blumenthal family, swept over the Prussian army. The victory was needlessly expensive, and the von Blumenthals were lucky all to have survived. But although 20,000 Prussians were lost to 12,000 French, the strategic gains were considerable. The Prussians had now cut the largest French army off from the rest of France. Nothing lay in their way to Paris. Bazaine retired into Metz again, where it took the Prussians a mere six corps to lock him in.

Bibliography

Elliot-Wright, Philipp	Gravelotte-St-Privat 1870, End of the Second Empire (1993)
Hooper, George	Sedan: The Downfall of the Second Empire (1887)
von Blumenthal, Count Hans	*Geschichte des Geschlechts derer Grafen und Herren von Blumenthal (1903)*
von Blumenthal, Dr. Robert	*Geschichte des Geschlechts derer Grafen und Herren von Blumenthal, Neubearbeitet und Erweitert* (unpublished)
von Rohr, H	*Aus der Geschichte des I. Garde-Dragoner-Regiments* (1898)
Wawro, Geoffrey	The Franco-Prussian War (2003)

www.ingramcontent.com/pod-product-compliance
Lightning Source LLC
Chambersburg PA
CBHW042014150426
43196CB00002B/45